Camion di immondizia
Colorare

Coloring Pages for Kids

Coloring Pages for Kids
An imprint of Ciparum LLC

Camion di immondizia Colorare
© 2017 Ciparum LLC
All rights reserved.
ISBN-10:1-63589-503-0
ISBN-13:978-1-63589-503-2

Coloring Pages for Kids

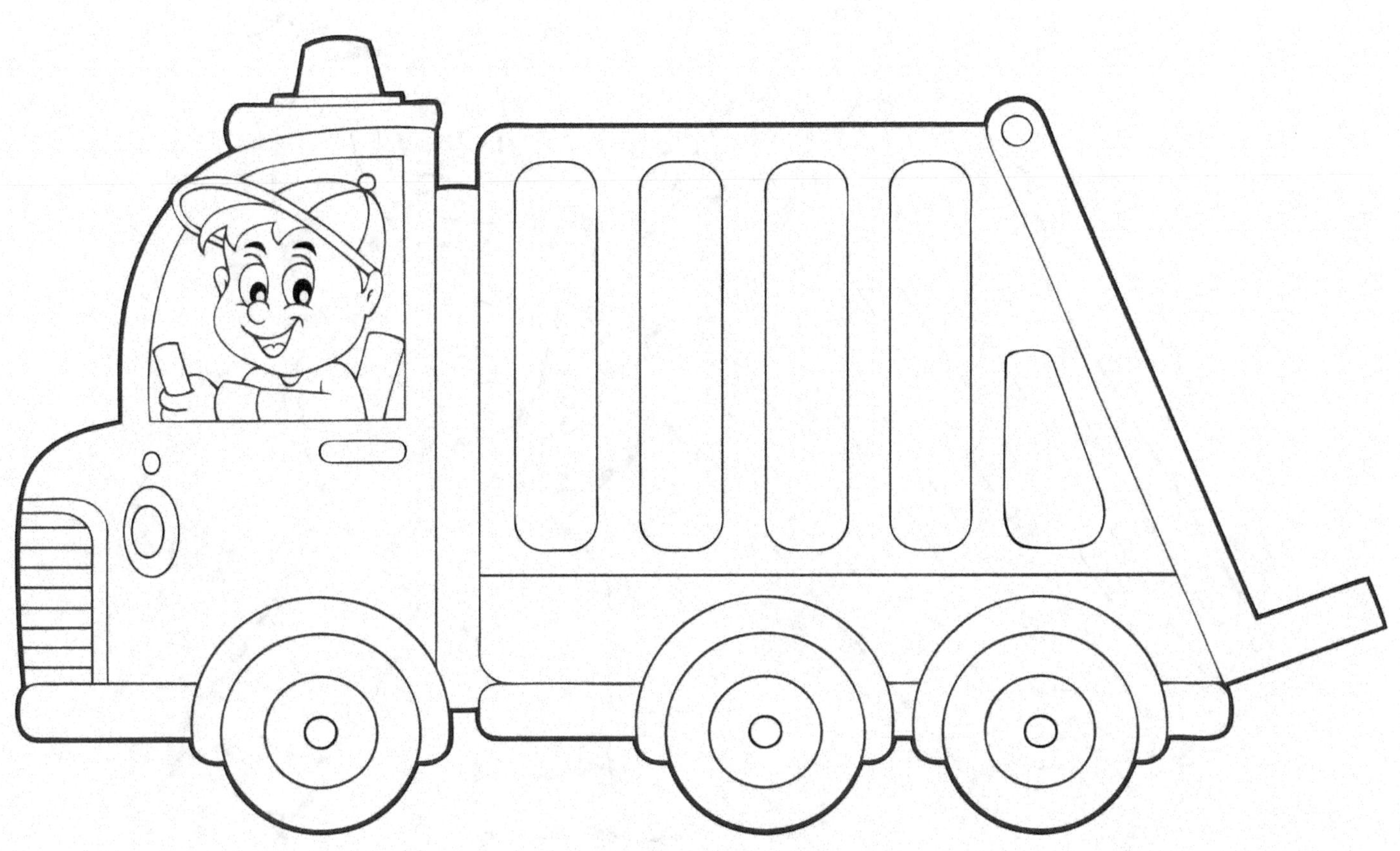

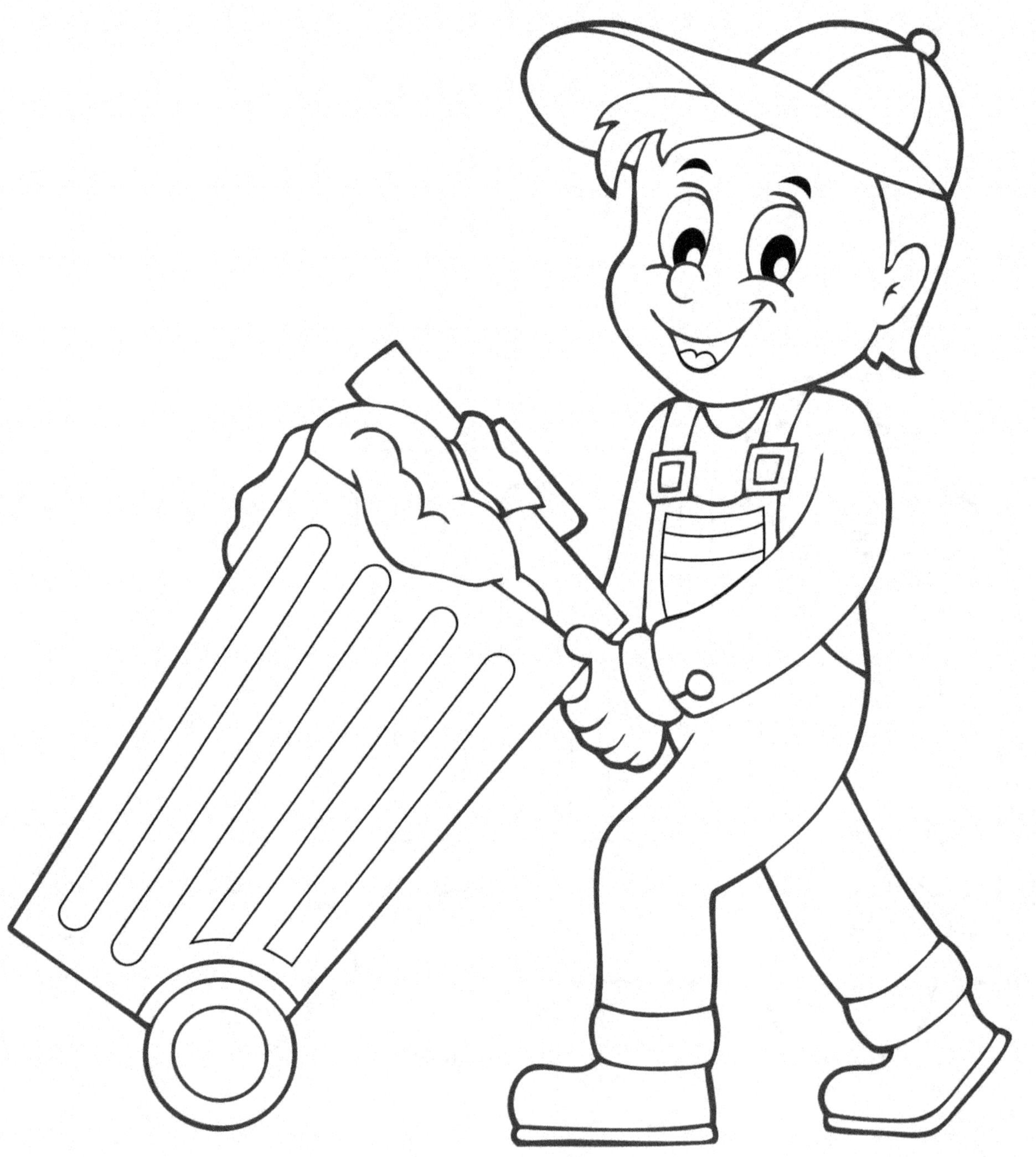

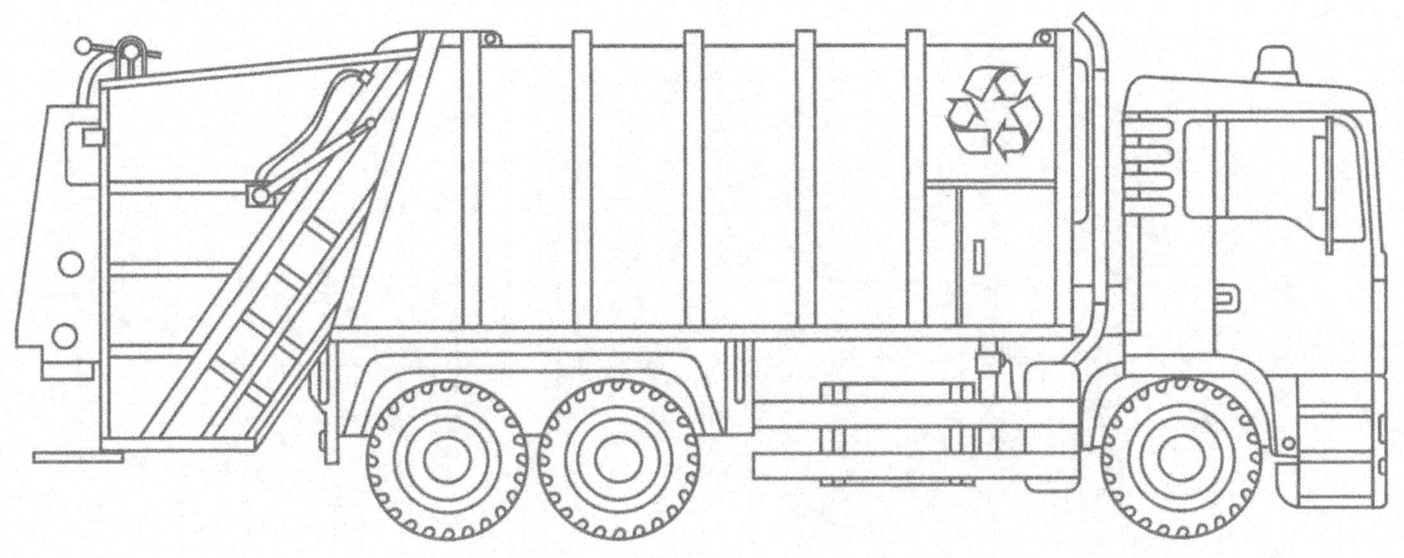

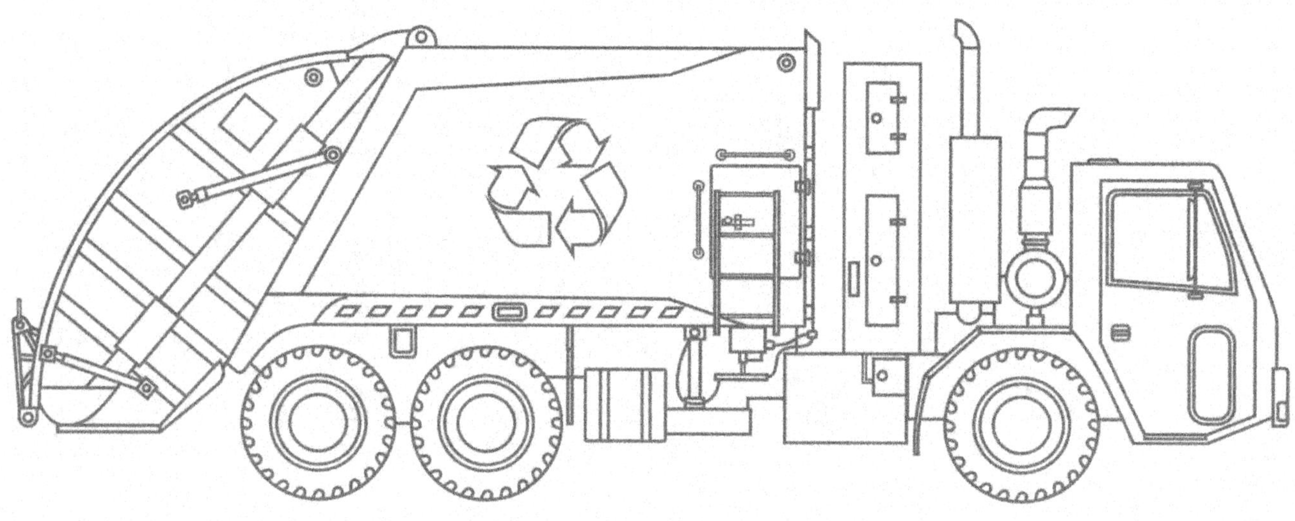

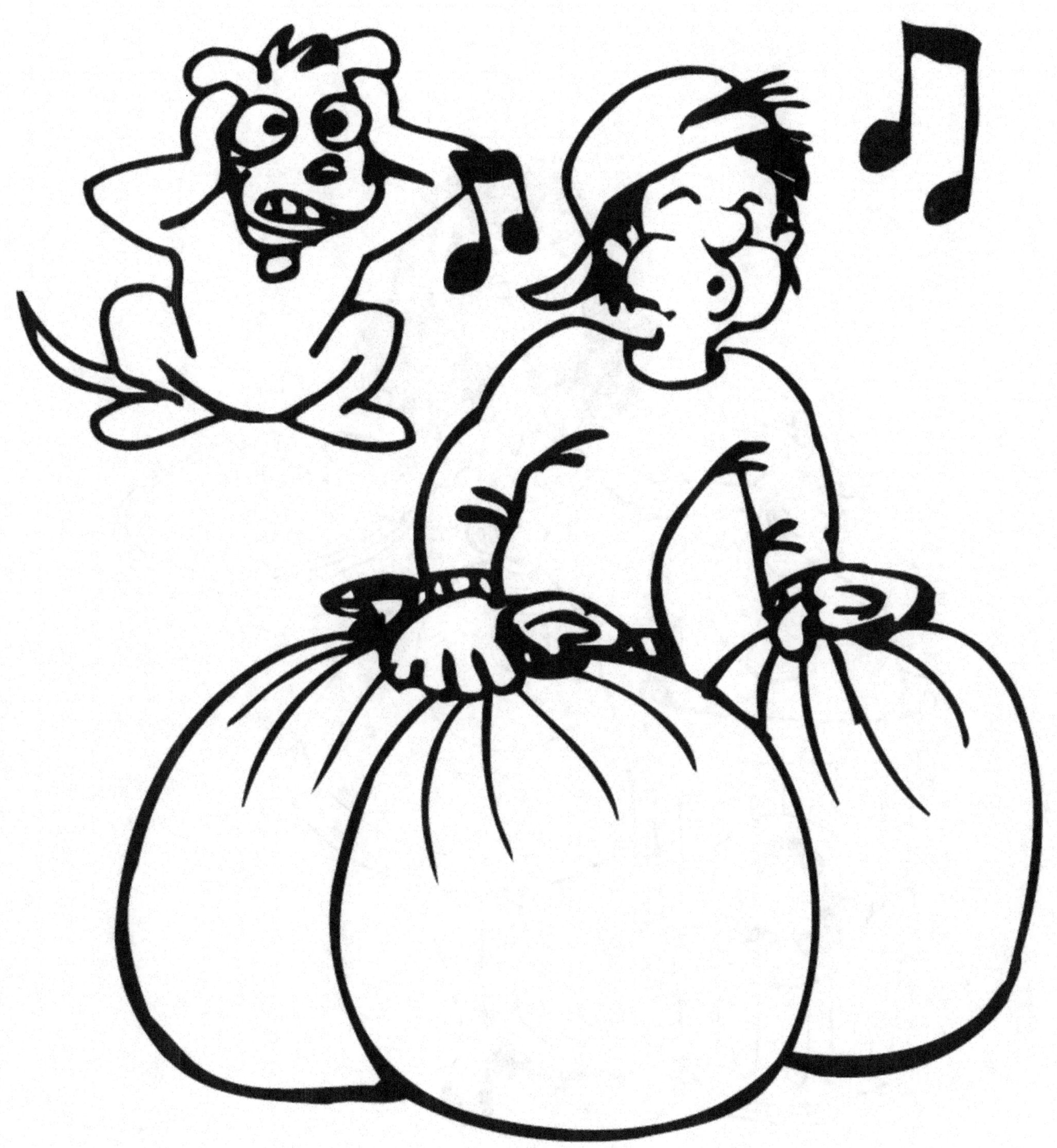

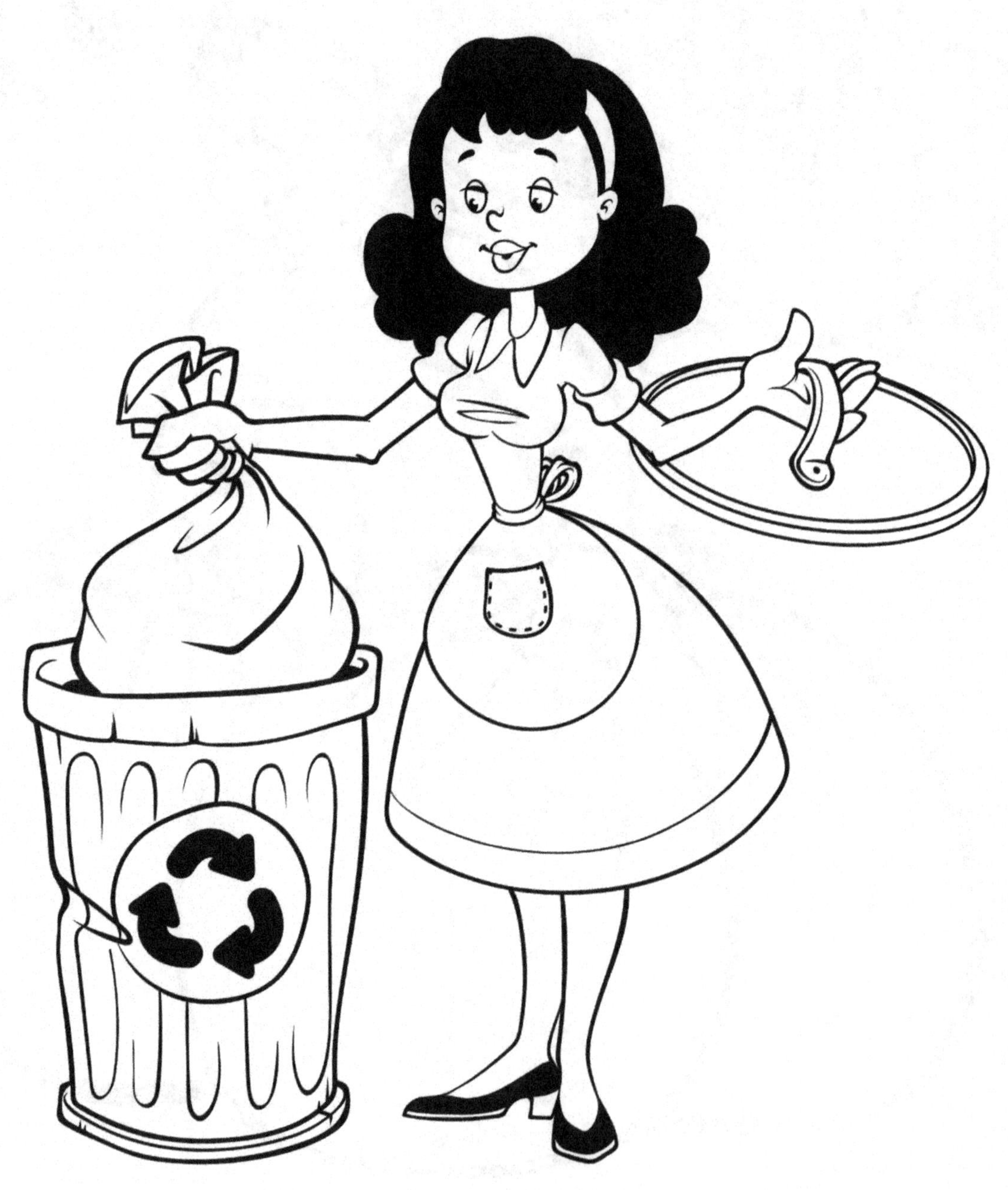

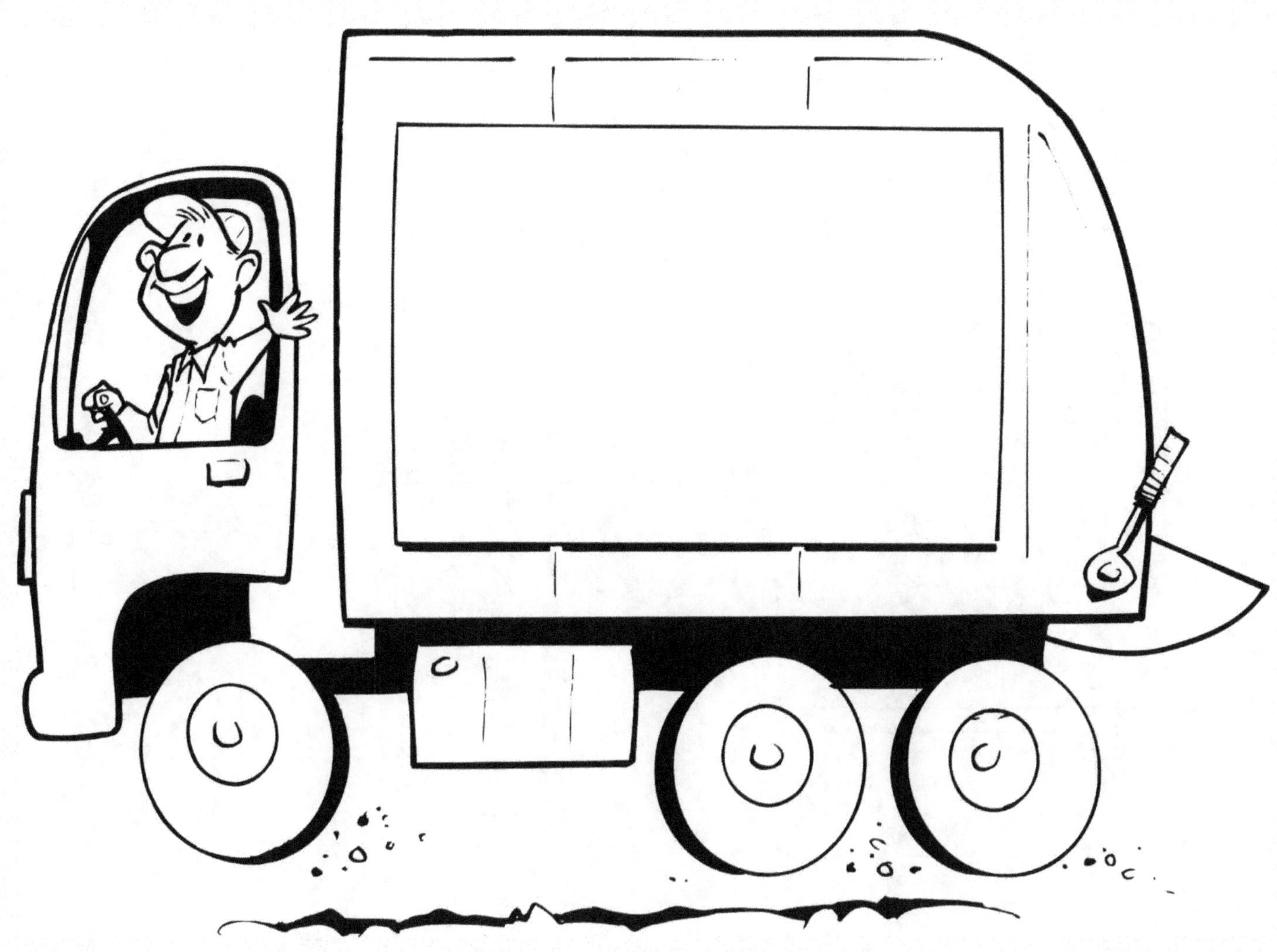

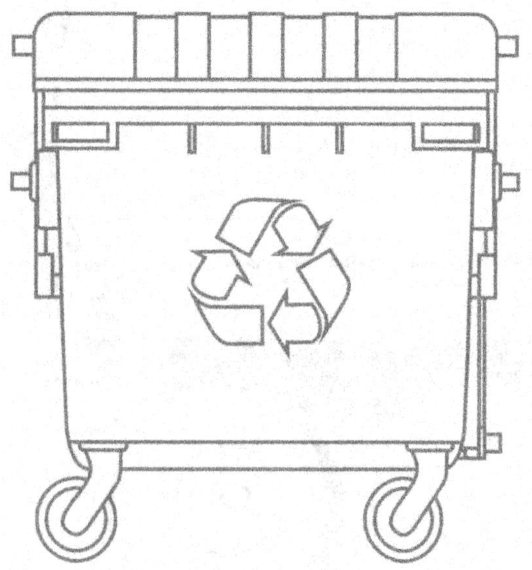 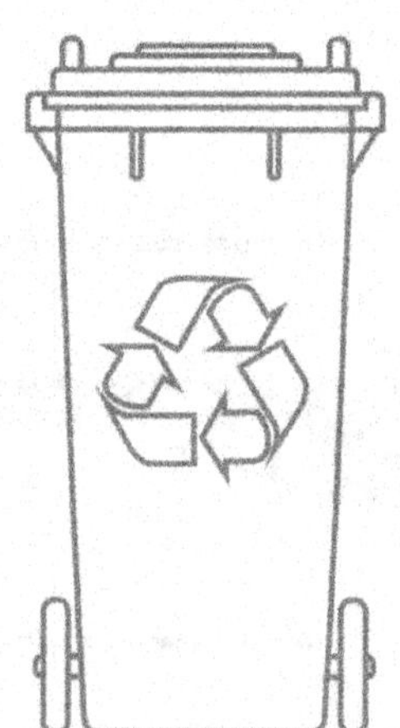 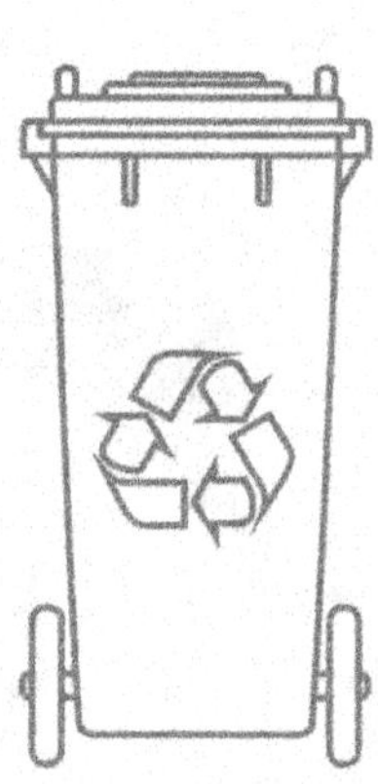

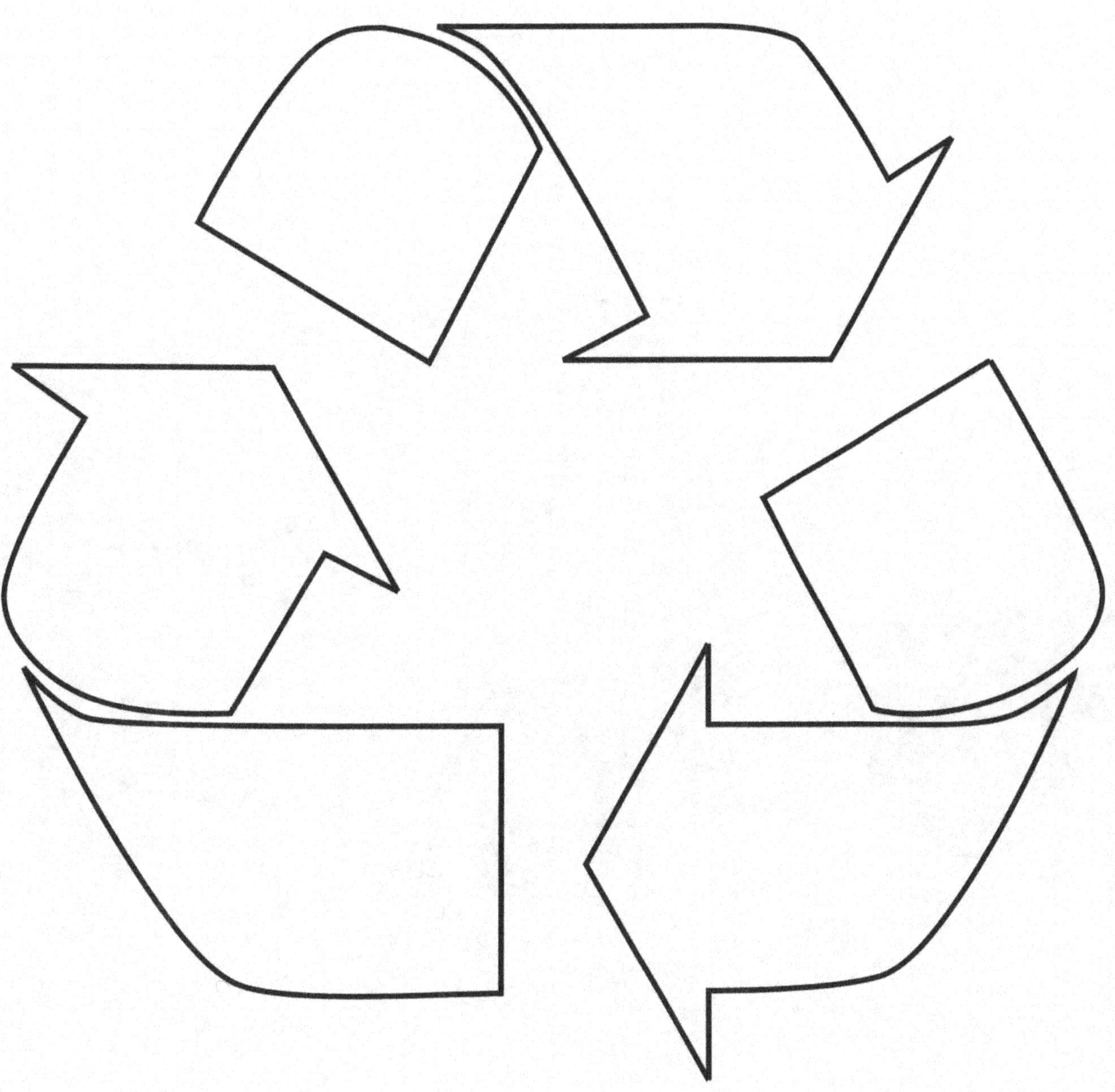

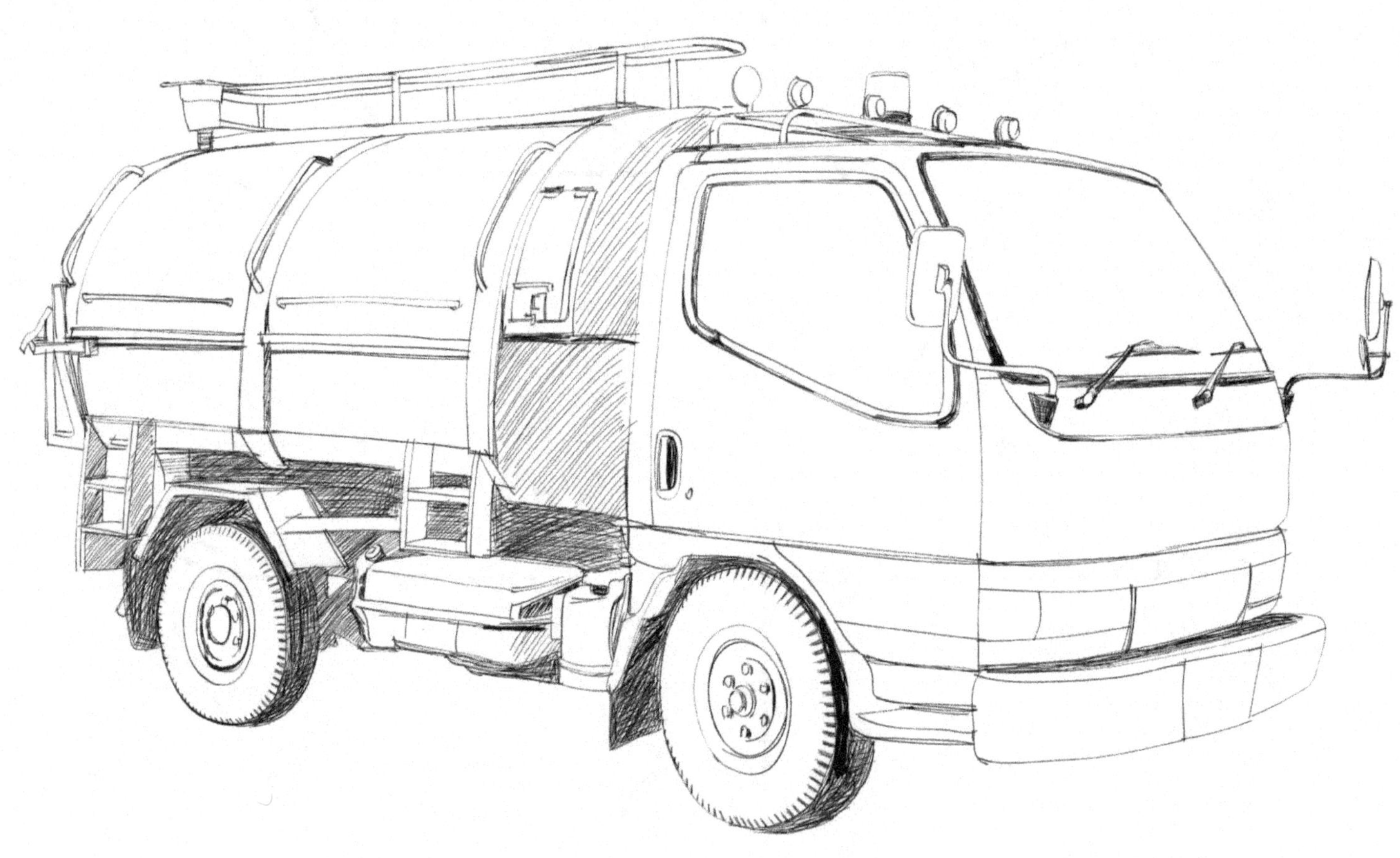

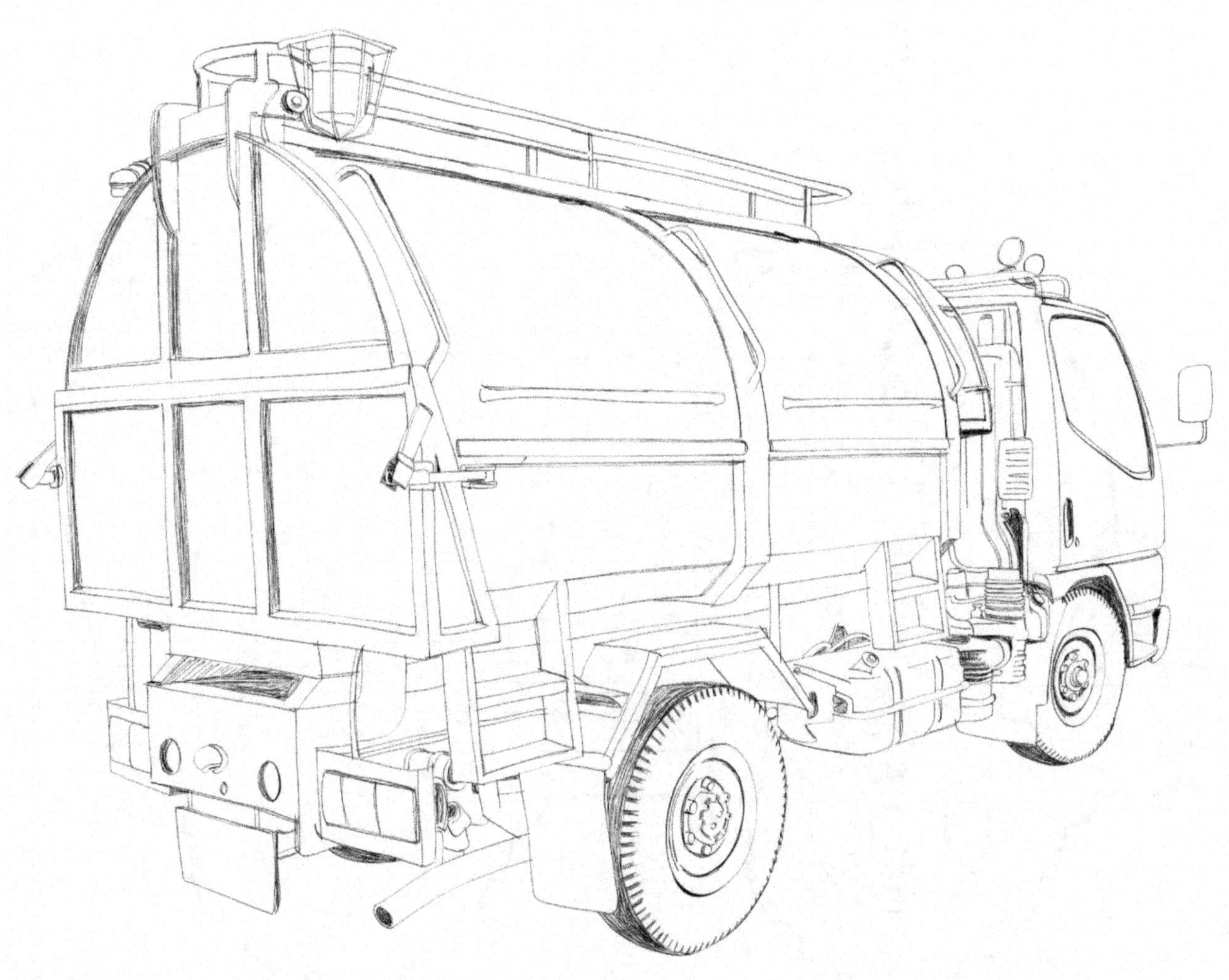

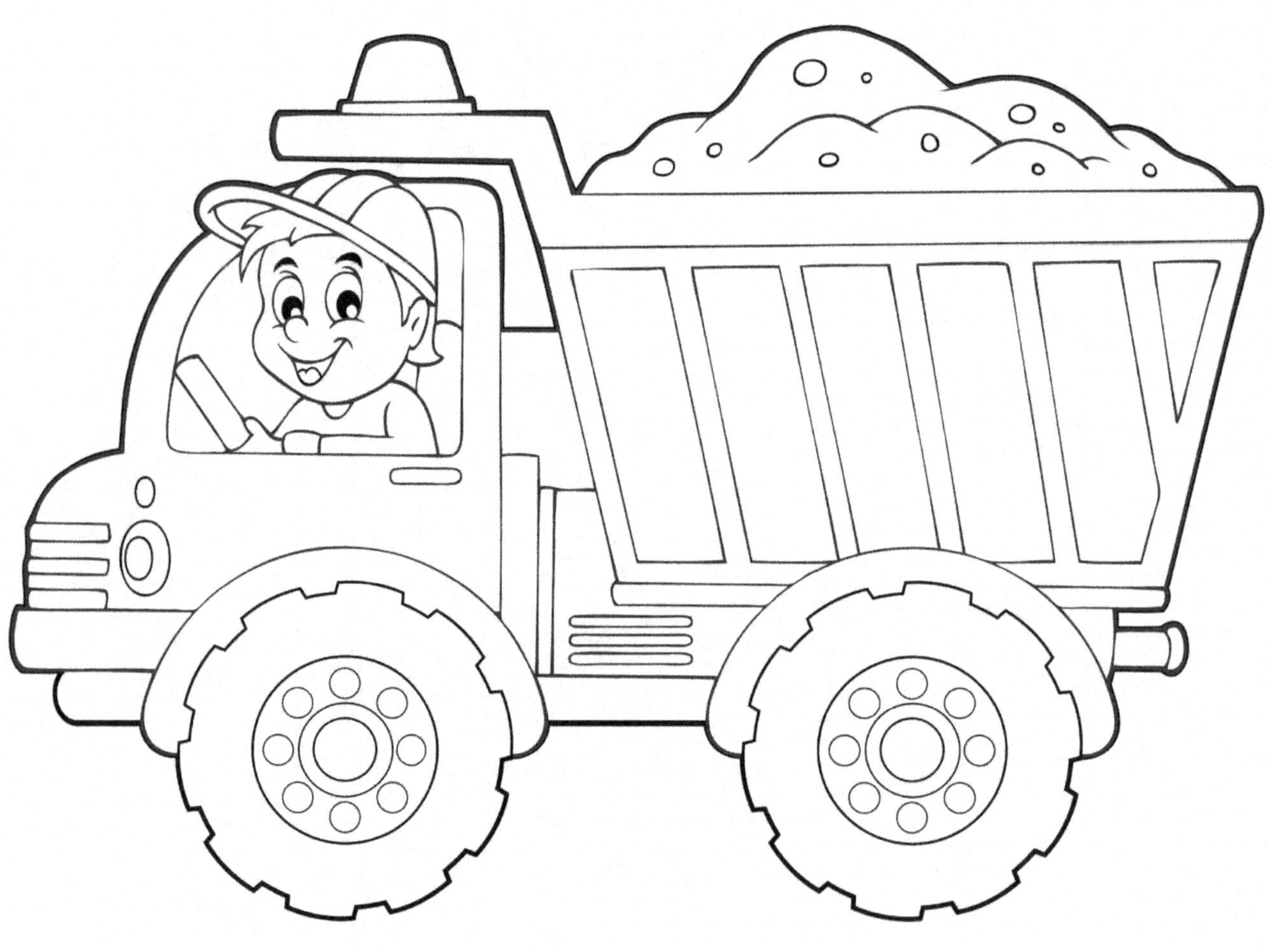

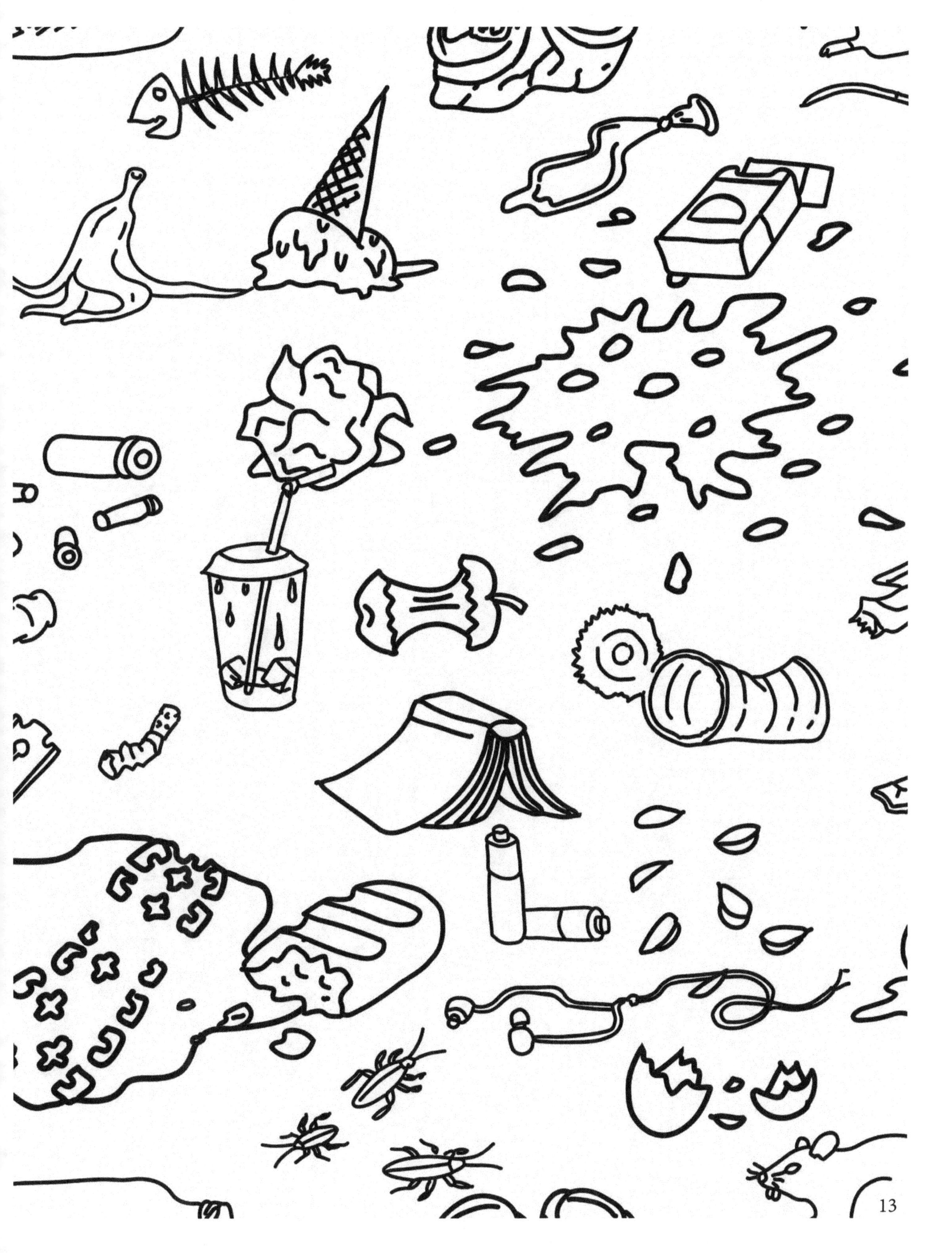

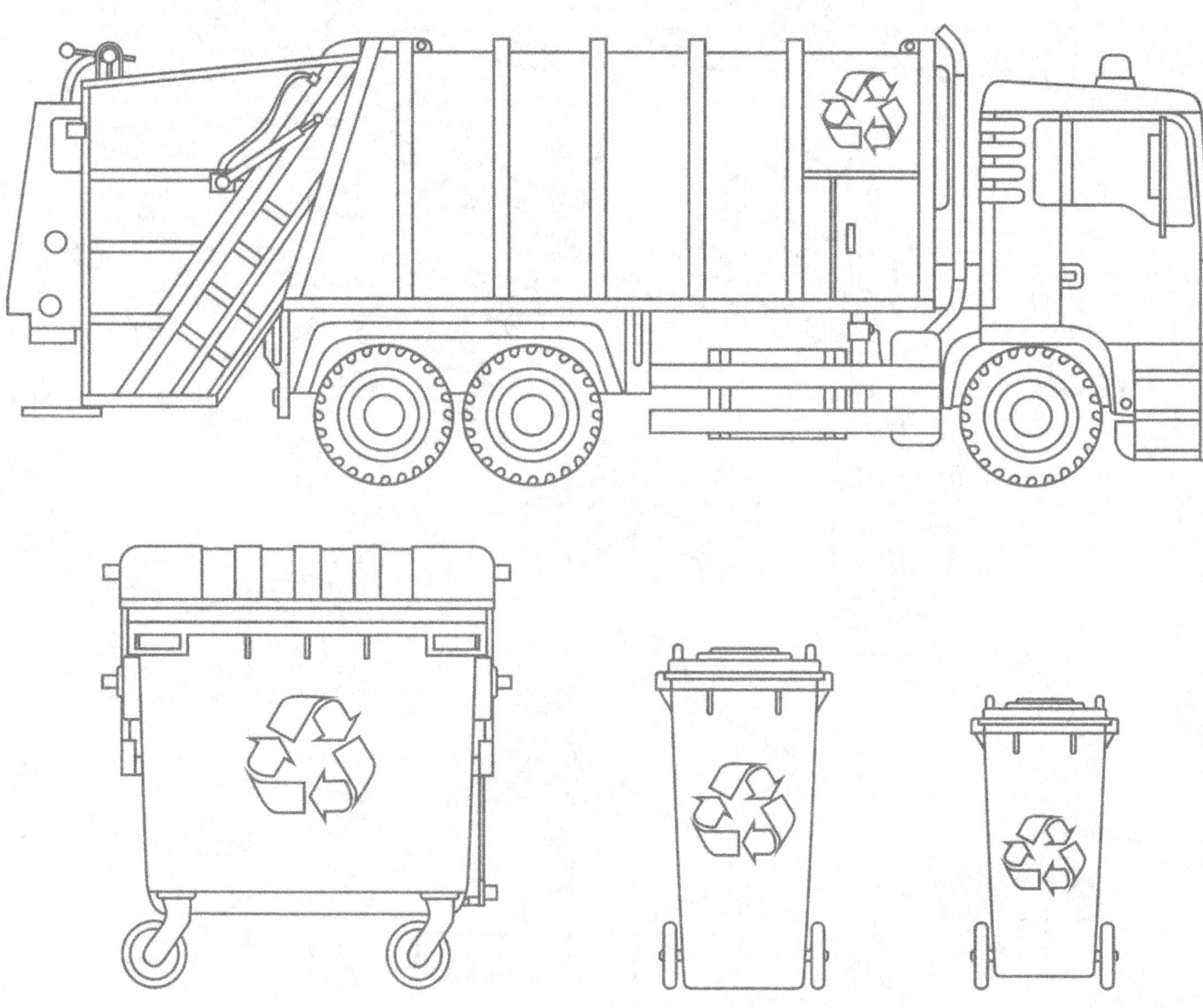

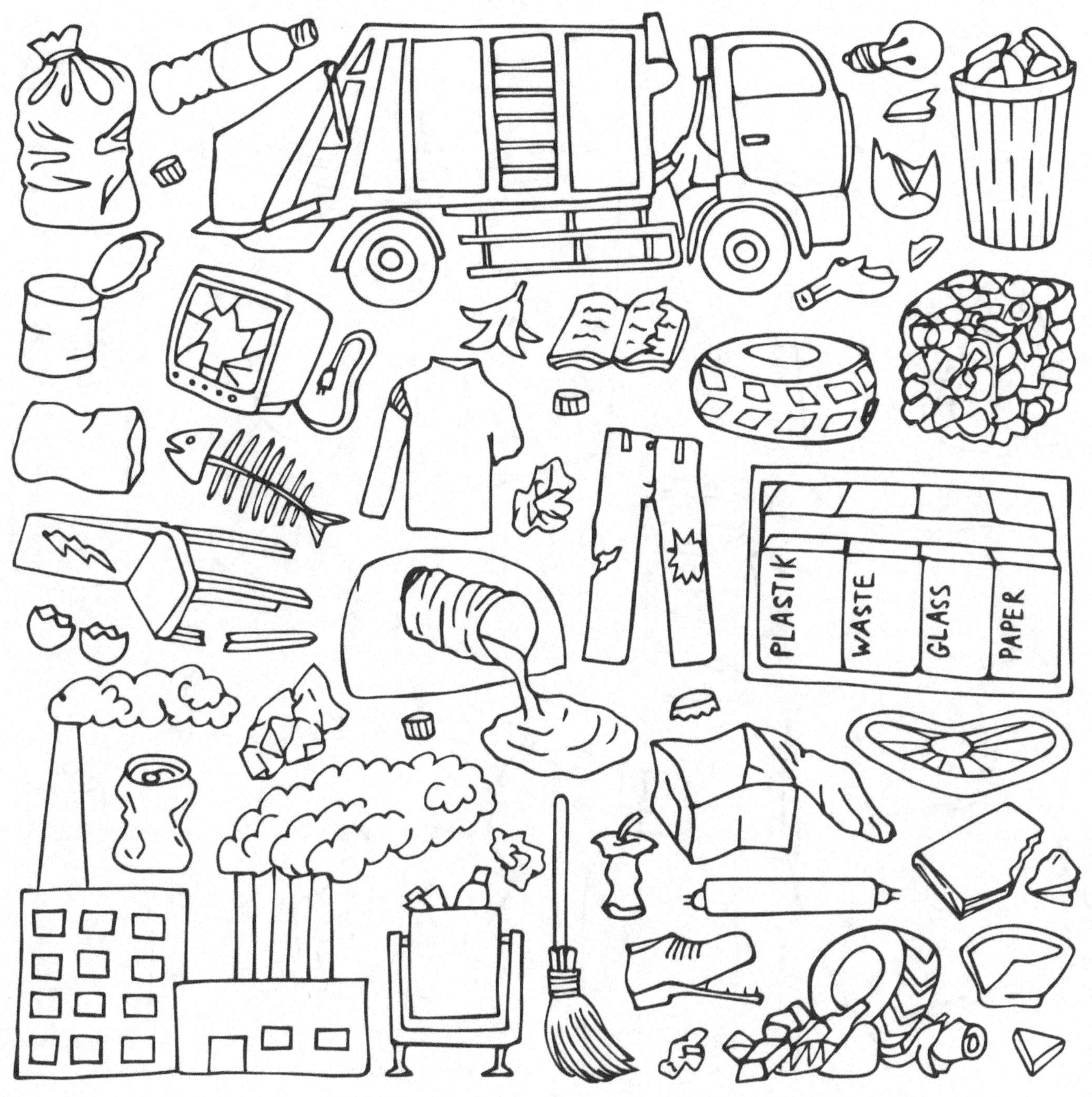

PLASTIK
WASTE
GLASS
PAPER

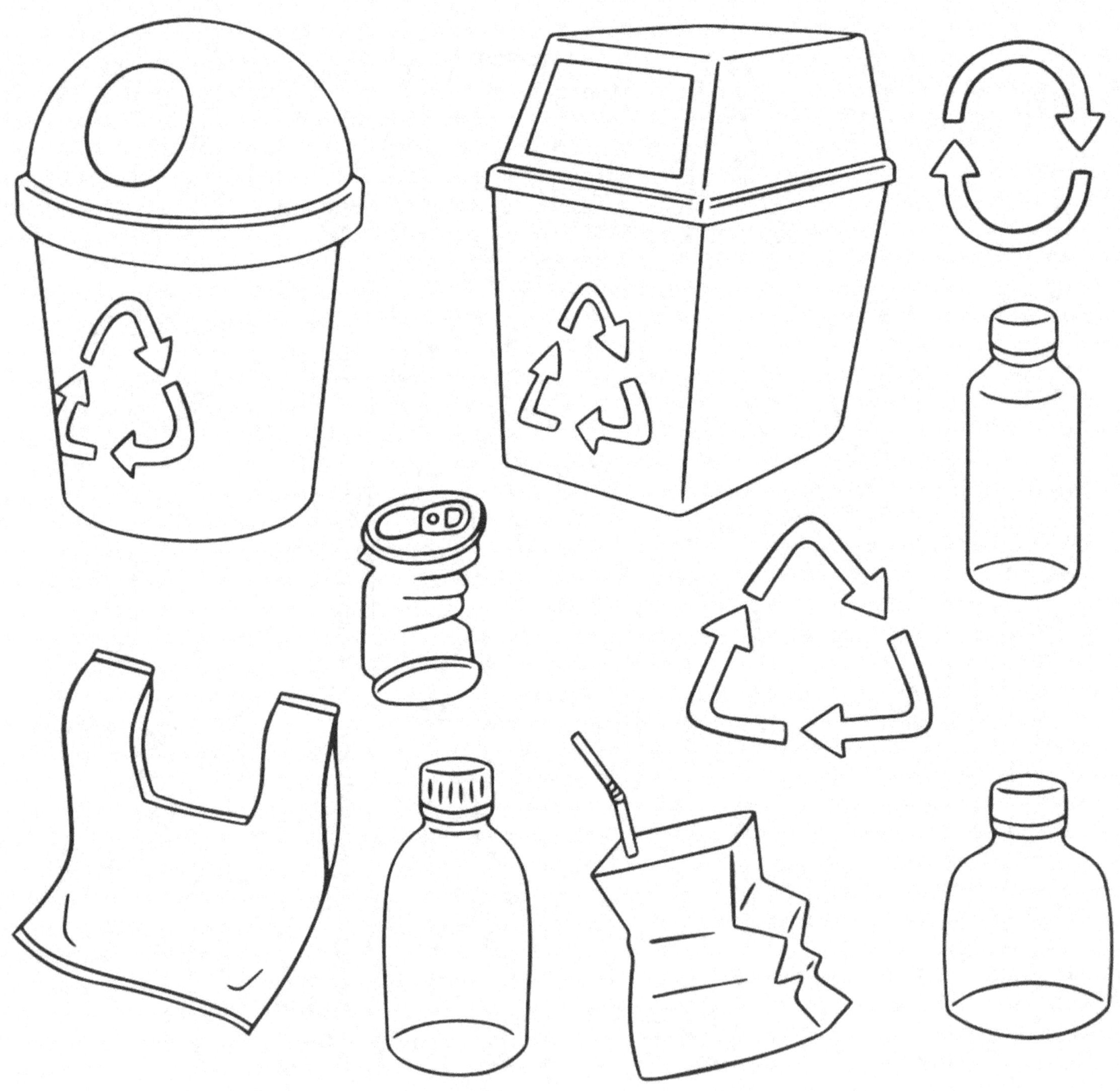

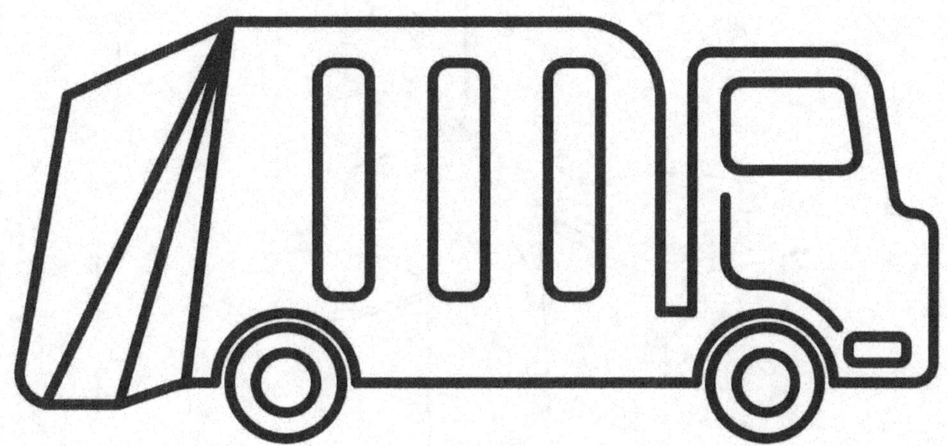

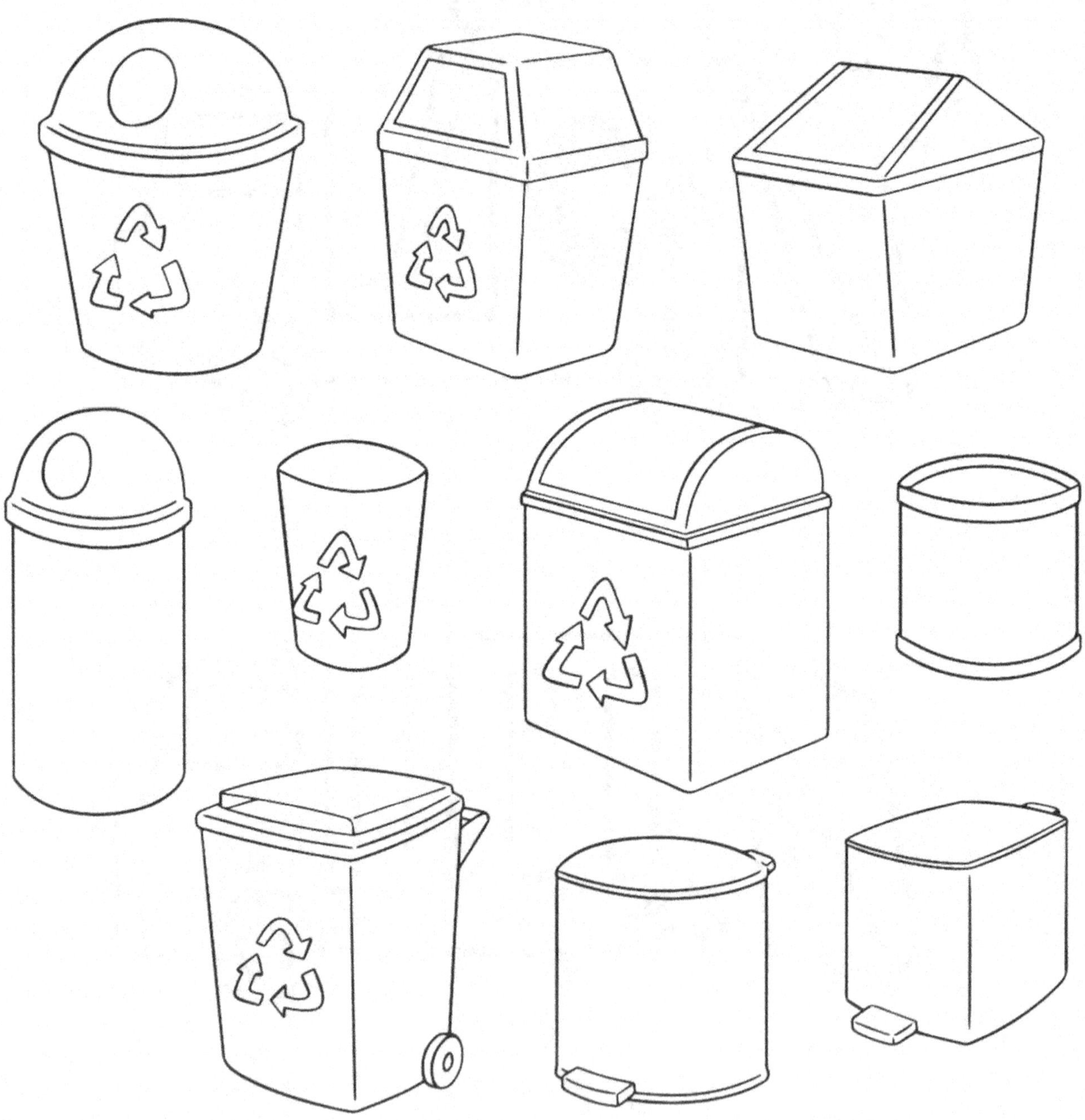

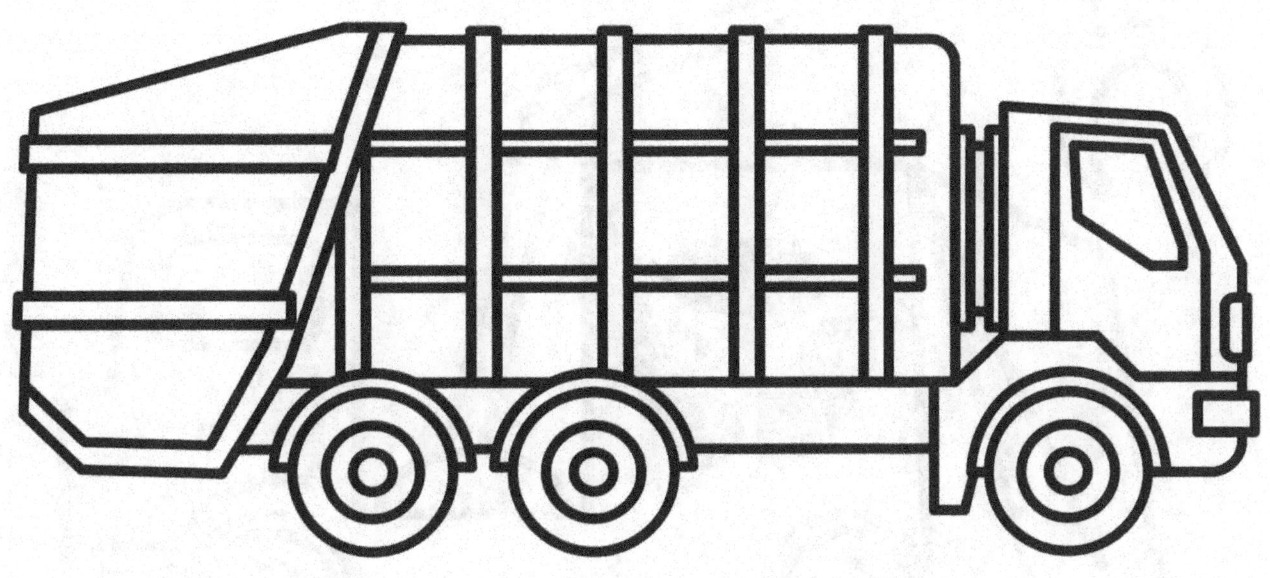

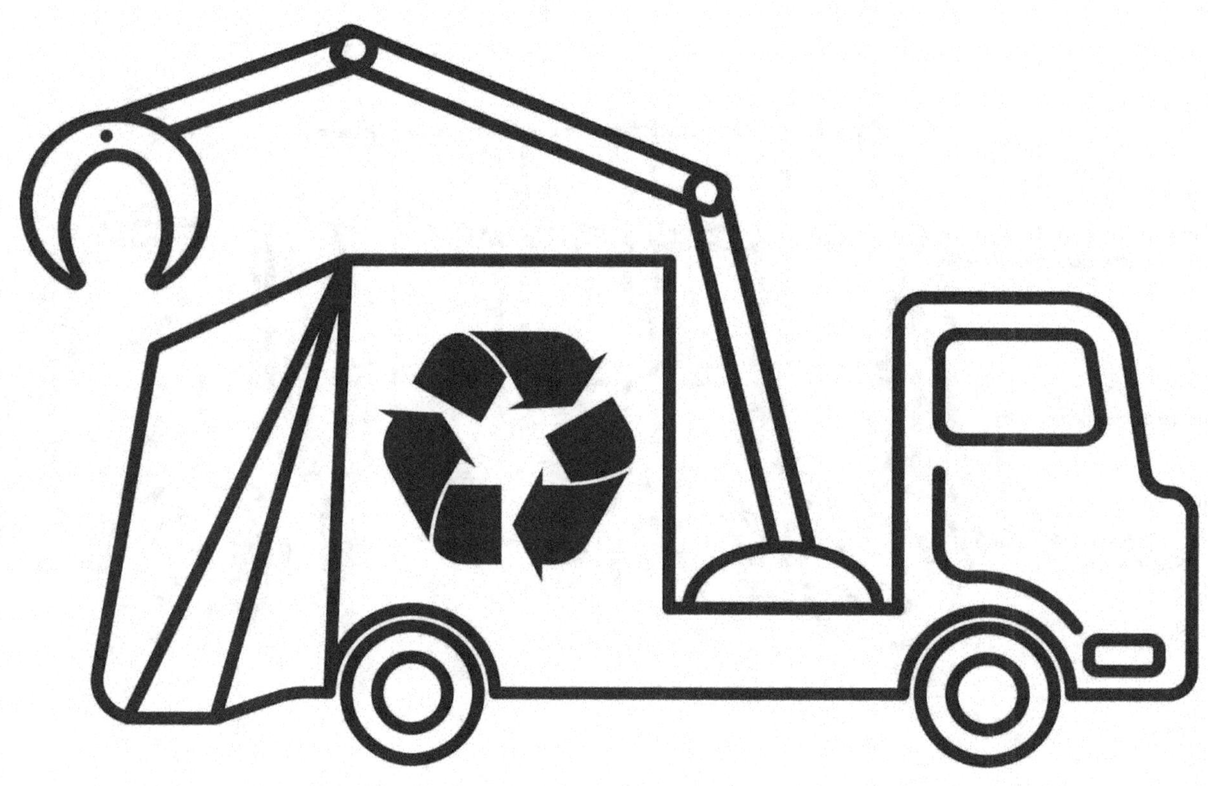

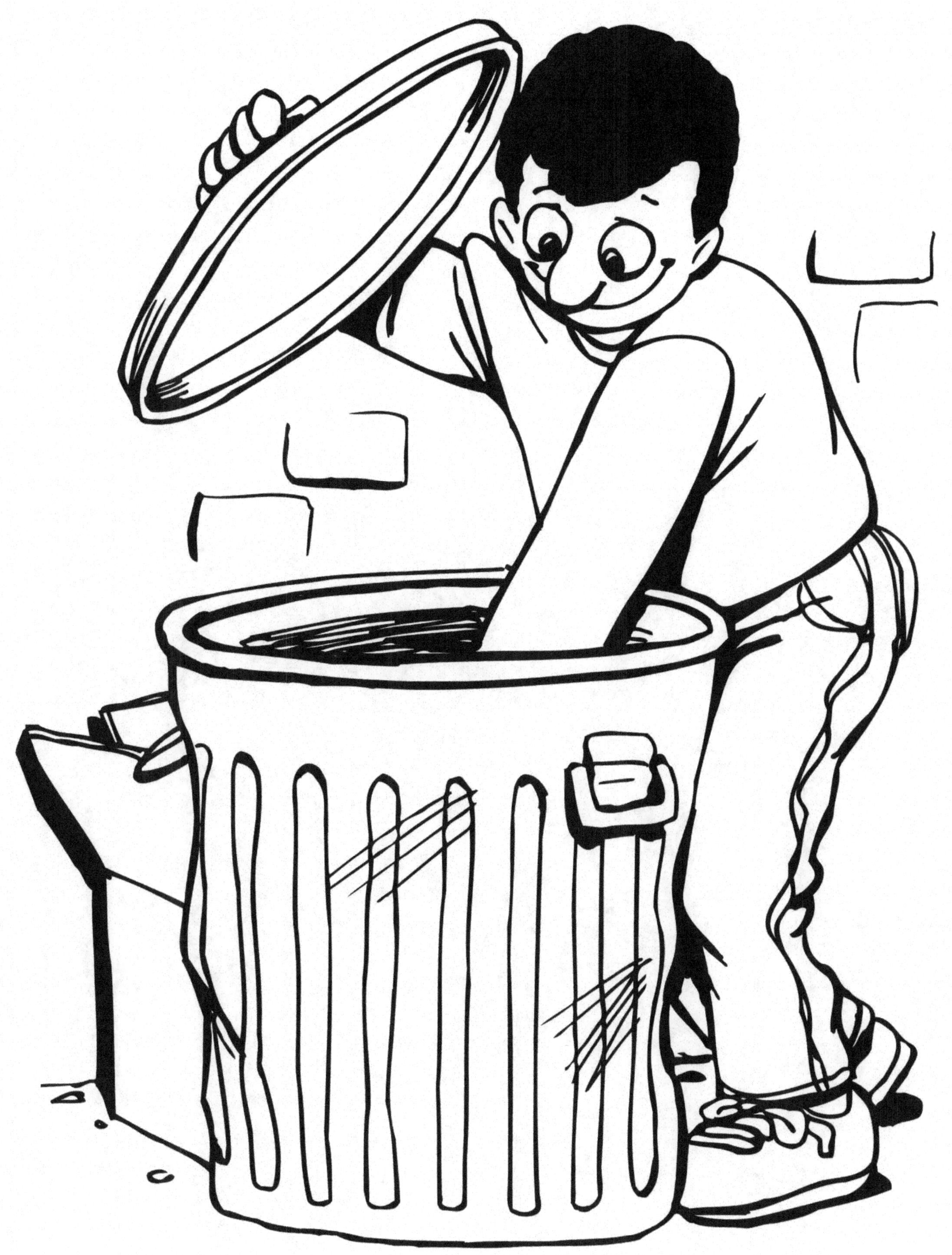

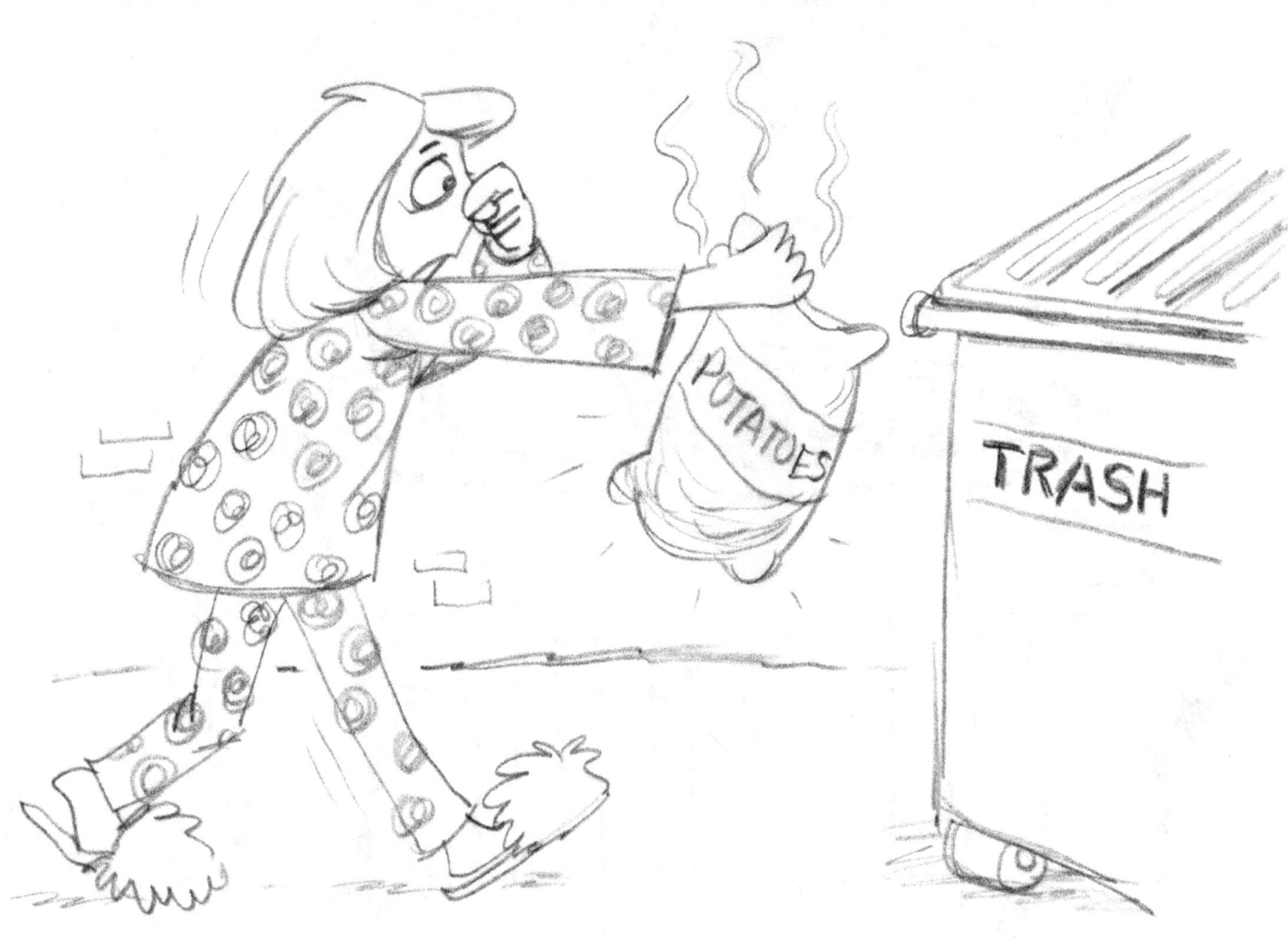

POTATOES
TRASH